Learning with Lulu
Chinese Mandarin

Level 1. Ages 6-13

跟鹿鹿学中文
第一册　　6 – 13 岁

Helen Wu

EasyMandarinUK®

Recommended by Hanban, the executive body of the Chinese Language Council International, an institution affiliated with the **Chinese Ministry of Education**

Introduction

Learning with Lulu – Chinese Mandarin (Level 1)

Learning with Lulu – Chinese Mandarin (with CD) is designed for children aged 6-13 for complete beginners to learn the foundation of Chinese Mandarin as a foreign language or anyone who would like to improve their Mandarin. Each book consists of a textbook with a CD. There are also flash cards for each level available separately as the supplementary material.

The book features a cartoon character called Lulu, a Chinese girl living in the UK. The sessions are written in themes according to Lulu's daily life with bright illustrations, lively songs, rhymes and games. You will find the book is easy to relate to and fun to learn.

The focus of this book:

- Conversation and listening
- Vocabulary and sentence construction
- Chinese character writing
- Phonetic symbols and tones

The themes included in this book:

- Greetings
- Courtesy words
- Self introduction
- Nationalities/countries
- Numbers and ages

- Colours
- Family members
- Body parts and illness
- Fruits shopping
- Animals

Contents

Lesson 1.   Lulu Goes to School

第一课.　　鹿鹿去上学
(lù lu qù shàng xué)

1. Let's Learn These New Words:

1. nǐ hǎo 你 好 hello	**2.** nǐ hǎo ma 你好 吗 how are you		
3. wǒ hěn hǎo 我 很 好 I am fine.	**4.** xiè xie 谢谢 thank you	**5.** zǎo ān 早 安 good morning

2. Imagine you are Lulu going to school, when you meet your teacher, what do you say to her?

3. Learn the Phonetic Symbols:

a   o   e

4. Can You Tell the Different Tones according to Lulu's Postures?

ā	á	ǎ	à
ō	ó	ǒ	ò
ē	é	ě	è

5. Can You Match them up?

	xiè xie
1) how are you	1) 谢 谢
	nǐ hǎo
2) hello	2) 你 好
	nǐ hǎo ma
3) I am fine	3) 你 好 吗
	zǎo ān
4) thank you	4) 早 安
	wǒ hěn hǎo
5) good morning	5) 我 很 好

6. Can You Read aloud and Write the Meaning in English under each box?

nǐ hǎo	nǐ hǎo ma

wǒ hěn hǎo	xiè xie

7. Let's Sing along:

xiǎo　xīng　xīng
小　星　星
Twinkle Twinkle Little Star

yì　shǎn　yì shǎn liàng　jīng jīng,
一　闪　一　闪　亮　晶　晶,
Twinkle, twinkle little star,

mǎn tiān dōu shì xiǎo xīng xīng,
满　天　都　是　小　星　星。
The sky is full of little stars.

guà zài tiān shàng fàng guāng míng
挂　在　天　上　放　光　明,
sparkling above the world so high,

hǎo xiàng xǔ duō xiǎo yǎn jīng
好　像　许　多　小　眼　睛。
look like many little eyes.

yì　shǎn yìshǎn liàng jīng jīng
一　闪　一　闪　亮　晶　晶,
Twinkle, twinkle little star,

mǎn tiān dōu shì xiǎo xīng xīng
满　天　都　是　小　星　星。
the sky is full of little stars.

8.　Can You Copy the Characters?

nǐ 你					
hǎo 好					

Lesson 2. Lulu in the Playground

dì èr kè

第二课.

lù lu zài cāo chǎng shàng

鹿鹿在操 场 上

1. Let's Learn These New Words:

1.	duì bu qǐ 对不起 I am sorry	**2.**	méi guān xi 没 关 系 It is OK./It doesn't matter.
3.	bú kè qi 不客气 You are welcome	**4.**	zài jiàn 再 见 goodbye

2. Before having dinner at home, can you say 'thank you' in Mandarin to your mummy for her cooking? Don't forget to say it this evening!

3. Learn the Phonetic Symbols:

i u ü

4. Can You Tell the Different Tones?

mī	mí	mǐ	mì
mū	mú	mǔ	mù
nū	nǘ	nǚ	nù

5. Can You Write down the Characters with These Symbols in this Lesson?

12

6. Can You Match the Words with Their Sounds?

1) 再见   2) 不客气   3) 谢谢   4) 对不起

1) bú kè qi   2) xiè xie   3) zài jiàn   4) duì bu qǐ

7. Can You Recognize the Characters and Draw Pictures accordingly?

wǒ
我

zài jiàn
再见

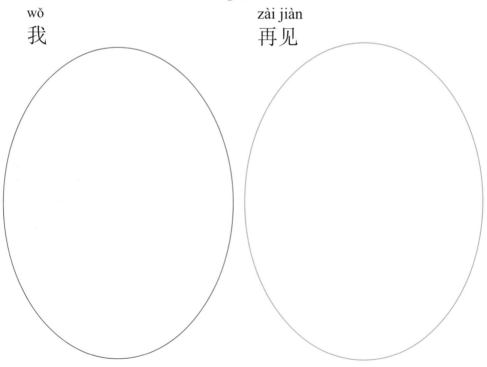

8. Let's Play a Game:

zhǎo   péng   you
找　朋　友
Looking For a Friend

zhǎo zhǎo   zhǎo péng you
找,　　找,　　找　朋　友,
Look, look, looking for a friend,

zhǎo dào yí gè hǎo péng you
找　到　一　个　好　朋　友。
I found a good friend.

jìng gè lǐ ya wò wò shǒu
敬　个 礼 呀 握 握 手,
Salute to you, shake hands with you,

nǐ   shì   wǒ de hǎo péng you
你　是　我　的　好　朋　友。
You are my good friend.

zài jiàn
再 见!
Goodbye!

Instructions: When you hear the words ‘敬 个 礼 呀 握 握 手’ (jìng gè lǐ ya wò wò shǒu), you need to salute and shake hands with your friends in the game.

9. Can You Copy the Characters?

kè 客					
qì 气					

Lesson 3. Lulu Meets New Friends I

dì sān kè

第三课.

lù lu yù jiàn xīn péng you   yī

鹿鹿遇见新 朋友 （一）

1. Let's Learn These New Words:

1.	shén me 什 么 what	2.	míng zi 名 字 name
3.	jiào 叫 to call/ to be called	4.	nǐ ne 你呢? What about you?

2. It is Your Turn:

Can you tell your friends what your surname is?

wǒ xìng
我姓_____。

Well Done! Now can you tell what your name is?

wǒ jiào
我叫_____。

Have you got a Chinese name?

_____

3. Learn the Phonetic Symbols:

b

p

m

f

4. Can You Read aloud?

bā	bá	bǎ	bà
pō	pó	pǒ	pò
mē	mé	mě	mè
fū	fú	fǔ	fù

5. Can You Match up the Right Words?

<table>
<tr><td>1)</td><td>shén
什</td></tr>
<tr><td>2)</td><td>míng
名</td></tr>
<tr><td>3)</td><td>nǐ
你</td></tr>
</table>

<table>
<tr><td>a)</td><td>me
么</td></tr>
<tr><td>b)</td><td>jiào
叫</td></tr>
<tr><td>c)</td><td>zi
字</td></tr>
</table>

6. Can You Tell Which Parts are the Same in These Characters? Write them Down.

你 什	

叫 吗	

6. Let's Sing along:

xiǎo yàn zi

小 燕 子
Little Swallow

xiǎo yàn zi chuān huā yī
小 燕 子, 穿 花 衣,
Little swallow, in floral dress,

nián nián chūn tiān dào zhè lǐ
年 年 春 天 到 这里。
Comes here every spring.

wǒ wèn yàn zi nǐ wèi shá lái
我 问 燕 子 你 为 啥 来?
I asked the swallow why you came?

yàn zi shuō zhè lǐ de chūn tiān zuì měi lì
燕 子 说:"这里 的 春 天 最美丽。"
She said," Spring here is the most
beautiful one."

6. Can You Copy the Characters?

shén 什					
me 么					

19

Lesson 4.   Lulu Meets New Friends II

dì sì kè   lù lu yù jiàn xīn péng you   èr
第四课.   鹿鹿遇见 新 朋友 二)

1. Let's Learn These New Words:

shì	nǎ	rén
1. 是	2. 哪	3. 人
to be	which	person/people
guó		zhōng guó
4. 国		5. 中 国
nation/country		China

2. Which Countries Have the Following Landmarks?

yīng guó	měi guó	zhōng guó	fǎ guó
英 国	美 国	中 国	法 国
Britain	America	China	France

3. Do You Know Why China is Called

中国 - zhōng guó?

4. Learn the Phonetic Symbols

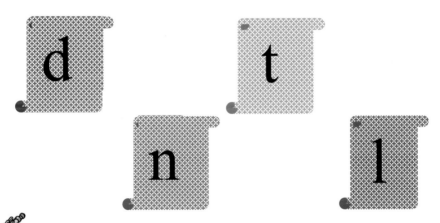

d

t

n

l

5. Can You Complete the Four Tones in Each Group?

dī	dí	dì
tē	tě	tè
nǘ	nǔ	nǜ
lū	lú	lǔ

6. Can You Match Them up?

yīng guó
英 国

zhōng guó
中 国

měi guó
美 国

rén
人

person/people

America

China

Britain

7. Draw Something Famous about Your Country and Explain:

8. Let's Recite a Poem:

é

鹅

Goose

é é é 鹅， 鹅， 鹅， Goose, goose, goose,	qū xiàng xiàng tiān gē 曲 项 向 天 歌. bending its neck and singing towards the sky.
bái máo fú lǜ shuǐ 白 毛 浮 绿 水， with her white feather floating on green water,	hóng zhǎng bō qīng bō 红 掌 拨 清 波. and red paws strolling the clear wave.

 9. Can You Copy The Characters?

zhōng 中					
rén 人					

Lesson 5. Lulu's Birthday Party

lù lu de shēng rì jù huì

第五课.   鹿鹿的生日聚会

1. Let's Learn These New Words:

jǐ	suì	jīn tiān
1. 几	2. 岁	3. 今天
how many	year	today
shēng rì	kuài lè	
4. 生 日	5. 快 乐	
birthday	happy	

2. Can You Count 1 - 10 with Chinese Sign Language?

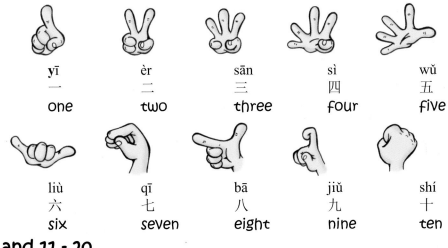

yī	èr	sān	sì	wǔ
一	二	三	四	五
one	two	three	four	five

liù	qī	bā	jiǔ	shí
六	七	八	九	十
six	seven	eight	nine	ten

and 11 - 20...

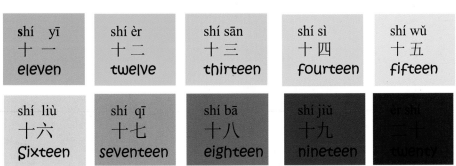

shí yī	shí èr	shí sān	shí sì	shí wǔ
十 一	十 二	十 三	十 四	十 五
eleven	twelve	thirteen	fourteen	fifteen

shí liù	shí qī	shí bā	shí jiǔ	èr shí
十 六	十 七	十 八	十 九	二 十
Sixteen	seventeen	eighteen	nineteen	twenty

3. Learn the Phonetic Symbols:

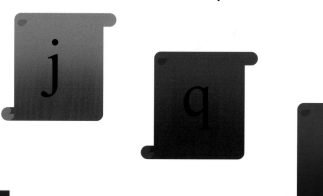

4. Can You Add the Right Tone Symbols according to Reading?

jia	jia	jia	jia
qi	qi	qi	qi
xu	xu	xu	xu

Note: When 'j', 'q' and 'x' are used with 'ü', 'ü' should be written as 'u'.

5. Can You Match Them up?

zhù	shēng	kuài lè	jǐ
birthday	wish	how many	happy

6. Tell Your Friends How Old You Are in Mandarin:

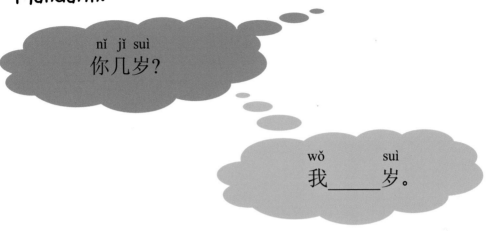

nǐ jǐ suì
你几岁?

wǒ　　　 suì
我＿＿＿岁。

7. Let's Sing along:

shēng rì kuài lè
生 日 快 乐
Happy Birthday

zhù nǐ shēng rì kuài lè
祝 你 生 日 快 乐,
Happy birthday to you,

zhù nǐ shēng rì kuài lè
祝 你 生 日 快 乐,
Happy birthday to you,

zhù nǐ shēng rì kuài lè
祝 你 生 日 快 乐,
Happy birthday to you,

zhù nǐ shēng rì kuài lè
祝 你 生 日 快 乐。
Happy birthday to you.

8. Can You Write Down the Number of Candles under Each Group?

Can You Copy These Characters?

shēng 生					
rì 日					

29

Lesson 6.   Lulu at the Florist

dì liù kè

第六课.

lù lu zài huā diàn

鹿鹿在花店

1. Let's Learn These New Words:

1.	xǐ huan 喜 欢 to like	2.	yán sè 颜 色 colour
3.	fěn hóng sè 粉 红 色 pink	4.	huā 花 flower

2. Would You Like to Know More Colours in Mandarin?

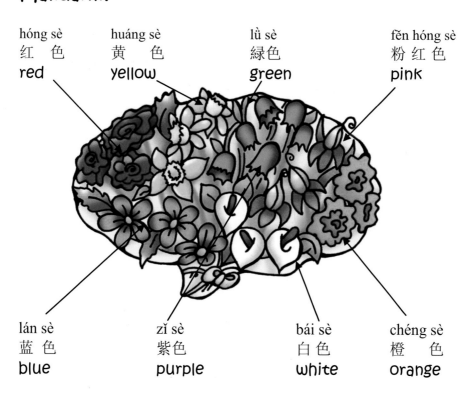

hóng sè
红 色
red

huáng sè
黄 色
yellow

lǜ sè
绿色
green

fěn hóng sè
粉 红 色
pink

lán sè
蓝 色
blue

zǐ sè
紫色
purple

bái sè
白 色
white

chéng sè
橙 色
orange

3. Learn the Phonetic Symbols:

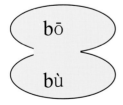 4. Can You Circle the Correct Sound in Each Group according to the Reading?

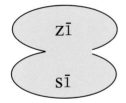

zī

sī

cǎi

zǎi

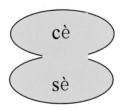

cè

sè

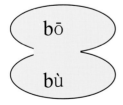

bō

bù

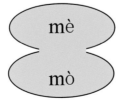

mè

mò

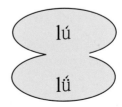

lú

lǘ

32

5. Can You Colour the Tulips and Explain the Colours in Mandarin?

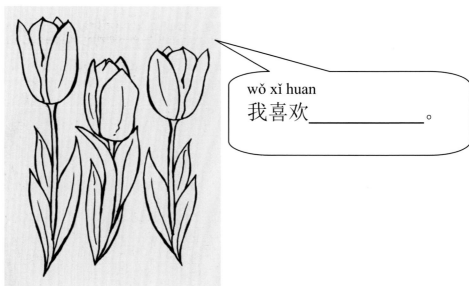

wǒ xǐ huan

我喜欢＿＿＿＿＿＿＿。

6. Let's Play a Game

Instructions 1:
Your friend lists one or two colours, you need to guess the animal that has those colours. For example, 黑 (hēi - black) and 白(bái -white), Panda

Instructions 2:
Your friend mentions one object, you need to tell which colour it is. For example, Clear sky - 蓝色 (lán sè - blue); Cloud - 白色 (bái sè -white).

7. Can You Copy the Characters?

hóng 红					
bái 白					

Lesson 7.   Lulu Visits Her Grandparents

dì qī kè

第七课.

lù lu kàn wàng yé ye nǎi nai

鹿鹿看 望爷爷奶奶

1. Let's Learn These New Words:

1.	nǎi nai 奶奶 grandma		2.	yé ye 爷爷 grandpa
3.	mā ma 妈妈 mum		4.	bà ba 爸爸 dad
5.	nǐ men 你们 you (more than one person)		6.	nín 您 you (used to show respects for senior people in the North)

2. Have You also Got These Family Members?

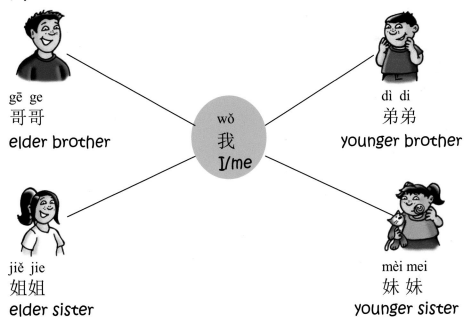

gē ge
哥哥
elder brother

dì di
弟弟
younger brother

wǒ
我
I/me

jiě jie
姐姐
elder sister

mèi mei
妹 妹
younger sister

3. Learn the Phonetic Symbols:

zh ch

sh r

4. Can You Tick the one being Read by the Teacher?

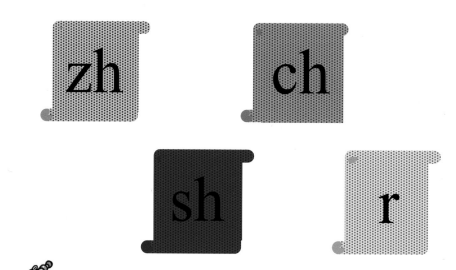

zhī	chí	shǐ	rì
zhú	chǔ	shù	rù
zhuó	chuò	shuō	ruò

5. Can You Tell Which Part is the Same in the Following Characters?

奶　　　妈　　　姐　　　妹

Hint: It is 女 – nǔ on the left hand side of the characters. It means woman/female.

5. Can You Read and Match?

nǎi nai 奶奶	grandma
yé ye 爷爷	elder brother
mèi mei 妹妹	grandpa
gē ge 哥哥	younger sister
jiě jie 姐姐	daddy
dì di 弟弟	mummy
bà ba 爸爸	elder sister
mā ma 妈妈	younger brother

6. Can You Make a Phone Call Today to Your Grandma and Greet Her in Mandarin?

7. Can You Copy the Characters?

mā 妈					
bà 爸					

Lesson 8. Lulu Visits the Doctor

dì bā kè
第八课.

lù lu qù kàn yī shēng
鹿鹿去看 医生

1. Let's Learn These New Words:

	nǎ er		bù		shū fu
1.	哪儿	2.	不	3.	舒服
	where		no/not		comfortable

	dù zi		téng
4.	肚子	5.	疼
	tummy		painful/aching/sore

 ## 2. Can You Name Other Parts of Your Body?

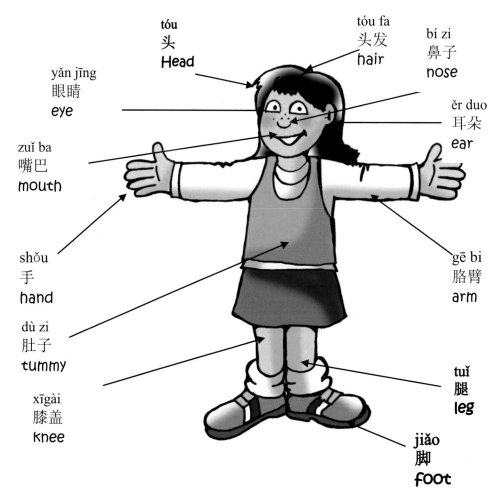

tóu
头
Head

tóu fa
头发
hair

bí zi
鼻子
nose

yǎn jīng
眼睛
eye

ěr duo
耳朵
ear

zuǐ ba
嘴巴
mouth

gē bi
胳臂
arm

shǒu
手
hand

dù zi
肚子
tummy

tuǐ
腿
leg

xīgài
膝盖
knee

jiǎo
脚
foot

3. Learn the Phonetic Symbols:

4. Can You Read aloud?

yā	yá	yǎ	yà
wū	wú	wǔ	wù

5. Can You Try to Read out the Tongue Twister?

shí sì shì shí sì,　　　sì shí shì sì shí.
十 四 是 十 四,　　　四 十 是 四 十.
shí sì bú shì sì shí　　　sì shí bú shì shí sì
十四不是 四十,　　　四十不 是 十 四.

5. Can You Draw the Correct Parts onto This Puppet according to Reading?

6. It is Your Turn:

Imagine you are the patient and your friend is the doctor, how do you tell her your health problem? Think about the body parts we just learned by using these sentences,

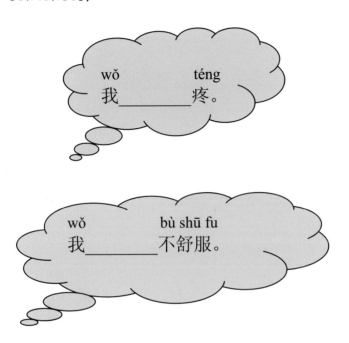

wǒ   téng

我＿＿＿＿疼。

wǒ   bù shū fu

我＿＿＿＿不舒服。

7. Can You Copy the Characters?

tóu 头					
shǒu 手					

Lesson 9. Lulu in the Supermarket

dì jiǔ kè   lù lu zài chāo jíshìchǎng
第九课.   鹿鹿在超 级市场

1. Let's Learn These New Words:

1.	yào 要 want	2.	píng guǒ 苹 果 apple
3.	hái 还 also	4.	xiāng jiāo 香 蕉 banana

2. Do You Want to Know More Fruits in Mandarin?

lí
梨
pear

cǎo méi
草 莓
strawberry

lǐ zi
李子
plum

jú zi
桔子
orange

yīng tao
樱 桃
cherry

máng guǒ
芒 果
mango

xī guā
西瓜
watermelon

bō luó
菠萝
pineapple

hā mìguā
哈蜜瓜
honeydew melon

4. Learn the Phonetic Symbols:

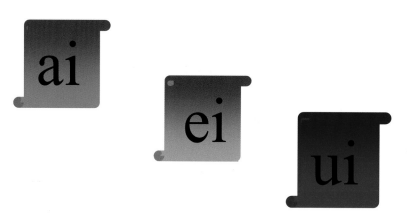

ai

ei

ui

5. Please Check the Positions of the Tones and Colour the Correct Apples in Red:

heī   zhuī   chūi   shuǐ

gěi   hūi   zaǐ   kāi

Hints: When adding tone symbols, always add on the top of 'a', if no 'a', then look for 'o','e','i' and 'u' in turn.

6. Show Time:

Instruction:
Actor A: Walking into a fruit market in Beijing
Actor B: Greeting and asking what fruit Actor A would like to buy.

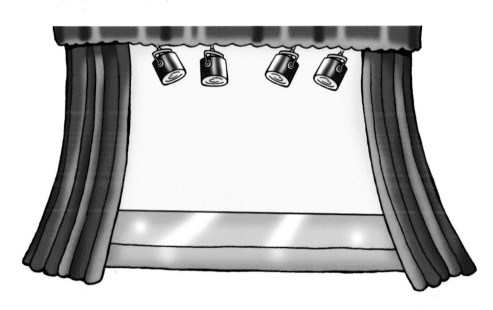

7. Can You Draw Your Favourite Fruits and Tell the name and its colour in Mandarin?

8. Let's Sing Along:

pāi pí qiú
拍皮球
Play the Ball

yī èr sān sān èr yī
一二三, 三二一,
One two three, three two one,

sì wǔ liù qī bā jiǔ
四五六, 七八九,
Four five six, seven eight nine,

yī èr sān sì wǔ liù qī
一二三四五六七。
One two three four five six seven.

dà jiā yì qǐ pāi pí qiú
大家 一起拍皮球。
Let's together play the ball.

9. Can You Copy the Characters?

píng 苹						
guǒ 果						

49

Lesson 10. Lulu in the Zoo

dì shí kè

第十课.

lù lu zài dòng wù yuán

鹿鹿在动物园

50

1. Let's Learn These New Words:

	dòng wù		cháng jǐng lù
1.	动物	2.	长 颈 鹿
	animal		giraffe
	zuì		ài
3.	最	4.	爱
	most		to love

2. Do You Know other Animals in the Zoo?

shī zi
狮子
lion

niú
牛
cow

lǎo hǔ
老虎
tiger

tù zi
兔子
rabbit

jīn yú
金鱼
gold fish

shé
蛇
snake

mǎ
马
horse

yáng
羊
sheep

hóu zi
猴子
monkey

jī
鸡
chicken

gǒu
狗
dog

zhū
猪
pig

51

3. Learn the Phonetic Symbols:

ao

ou

iu

4. Can You Read and Match?

lǎo hǔ

nǎi niú

hóu zi

5. Let's Play a Game:

Instructions:

You stand in front of your friends and imitate an animal. Let your friends guess what the animal is and say it in Mandarin.

6. Can You Fill in the Blanks to Form the Taught Animals?

hóu

猴_____

lǎo

老_____

jīn

金_____

tù

兔_____

m_____

zh_____

sh_____

ni_____

7. Let's Sing along:

liǎng zhī lǎo hǔ
两 只 老 虎
Two Tigers

liǎng zhī lǎo hǔ liǎng zhī lǎo hǔ
两 只 老 虎, 两 只 老 虎,
Two tigers, two tigers,

pǎo de kuài, pǎo de kuài,
跑 得 快, 跑 得 快。
Running fast, running fast.

yì zhī méi yǒu yǎn jīng
一只 没 有 眼 睛,
One with no eyes,

yì zhī méi yǒu wěi ba
一只 没 有 尾 巴,
The other with no tail,

zhēn qí guài zhēn qí guài
真 奇怪, 真 奇怪。
How strange, how strange.

 8. Can You Copy the Characters?

niú 牛					
yáng 羊					

54

Pin-in Chart
拼音

Initials 声母:

b	p	m	f	d
t	n	l	g	k
h	j	q	x	zh
ch	sh	r	z	c
s	y	w		

Finals 韵母:

a	o	e	i	u
ü	ai	ei	ui	ao
ou	iu	ie	üe	er
an	en	in	un	ün
ang	eng	ing	ong	

Combinations:

zhi	chi	shi	ri	zi
ci	si	yi	wu	yu
wa	wo	wai	wei	wan
wen	wang	weng	ya	ye
yue	yao	yuan	yin	yun
yan	ying	yong		

Note:

1. ü: when there is no initial in front of it, it is written as: yu, yue, yuan, yun; omit the two dots. When combining with a final, it is written as nü, lü.

2. iou, uei, uen: when adding an initial in front of them, they are written as iu, ui, un. For instance, liu, gui, and lun.

Certificate

**Congratulations
to ....(Name)**

**for successfully completing
this book.**

Well done!

Age...............................

Date................................